UNEARTHING ANCIENT CIVILIZATIONS

ANCIENT ROME REVEALED

BY DONNA REYNOLDS

Cavendish Square
New York

Published in 2023 by Cavendish Square Publishing, LLC
29 E. 21st Street, New York, NY 10010

First Edition

Website: cavendishsq.com

Library of Congress Cataloging-in-Publication Data

Names: Reynolds, Donna, author.
Title: Ancient Rome revealed / by Donna Reynolds.
Description: New York : Cavendish Square Publishing, [2023] | Series: Unearthing ancient civilizations | Includes index.
Identifiers: LCCN 2021051685 | ISBN 9781502666109 (library binding) | ISBN 9781502666086 (paperback) | ISBN 9781502666093 (set) | ISBN 9781502666116 (ebook)
Subjects: LCSH: Rome–Civilization–Juvenile literature.
Classification: LCC DG77 .R49 2023 | DDC 937–dc23/eng/20211023
LC record available at https://lccn.loc.gov/2021051685

Editor: Jennifer Lombardo
Copyeditor: Abby Young
Designer: Deanna Paternostro

The photographs in this book are used by permission and through the courtesy of: Cover, back cover Kristopher Kettner/Shutterstock.com; p. 4 Krisztian Juhasz/Shutterstock.com; p. 7 Lebrecht Music & Arts/Alamy Stock Photo; pp. 8–9 ColorMaker/Shutterstock.com; pp. 10, 14 Peter Hermes Furian/Shutterstock.com; p. 13 Everett Collection/Shutterstock.com; p. 16 Jeff Dalton/Shutterstock.com; p. 19 Hi-Story/Alamy Stock Photo; p. 20 Abel Halasz/Shutterstock.com; p. 22 Francesco Todaro/Shutterstock.com; p. 24 North Wind Picture Archives/Alamy Stock Photo; p. 26 Antiqua Print Gallery/Alamy Stock Photo; p. 28 (top left) Viacheslav Lopatin/Shutterstock.com; p. 28 (top right) Dave Head/Shutterstock.com; p. 28 (bottom) S.Borisov/Shutterstock.com.

CPSIA compliance information: Batch #CSCSQ23: For further information, contact Cavendish Square Publishing LLC, New York, New York, at 1-877-980-4450.

Printed in the United States of America

CONTENTS

This statue shows the wolf who became the mother of Romulus and Remus, according to legend.

CHAPTER ONE

A GROWING CIVILIZATION

The city of Rome began as several small villages built on hills near the Tiber River in Italy around 800 BCE. Over time, these villages joined together into a larger city. Around 753 BCE, this city was given the name Rome.

A MYTHICAL BEGINNING

According to ancient stories, Rome was founded by twin brothers named Romulus and Remus. They were the sons of Mars, the Roman god of war, and they were raised by a wolf. The brothers wanted to build a city, but they fought over where to do it. Romulus killed Remus, made himself king, and named the city "Rome" after himself.

The real story of Rome's beginning is not clear because this story is the one the Romans told each other. They did not write down their history, and the only books about Rome's early history were written years after the events happened. However, experts do know that seven kings ruled Rome between 753 and 509 BCE. **Archaeologists** have found items in Rome from this time that say "rex," which means "king" in Latin.

A ZOMBIE LANGUAGE

The early Roman language, Latin, is now a dead language. This means there is nowhere in the world where people grow up speaking Latin, and it cannot change over time. However, like a zombie, it's still around even though it's dead! Plants and animals all have a Latin name as well as a common name. For example, *Tyrannosaurus rex* means "terrible lizard king." Latin words are also used in law and politics.

POWER TO THE PEOPLE

In 509 BCE, the seventh king of Rome was overthrown. Instead of a monarchy, or a government ruled by a king, Rome became a republic. The people of Rome held the power, and they elected people to the government to make the laws citizens wanted.

Instead of a king or a president, the Roman Republic's leaders were called consuls. Two of them were elected every year. They worked with a governing body called the Senate. Senators were elected for life. The consuls also led the army during times of war.

Roman society was made of two groups. Patricians were people in the rich, land-owning upper class. Plebeians were the ordinary citizens who made up the lower class. Only wealthy people ended up being part of the Senate. This meant it was mostly the patricians who had power, while the plebeians had very few rights.

This picture shows Roman senators gathered to discuss politics.

MAKING THE LAWS

Around 450 BCE, Rome created its first written code of laws. It was carved onto 12 bronze tablets. These were called the Twelve Tables, and they were on display in the Forum. The Roman Forum was a place in the middle of the city where people could meet. It was where important political, religious, and social activities happened. Putting the Twelve Tables here made sure everyone knew the laws because everyone went to the Forum.

The Forum (*shown here*) was not inside a building. It was a place where people could gather outside.

Today, the ancient Forum is a very popular place for visitors to see. The word "forum" has also become part of the English language. It does not always refer to an actual place anymore. Instead, it can be any meeting, such as a space online, where people are allowed to share their ideas openly—just like they did in the Roman Forum.

The city of Rome was in the middle of what is now the country of Italy. Today, Rome is the country's capital city, as shown here.

CHAPTER TWO

EXPANDING THE REPUBLIC

Around the end of the 5th century BCE, the Roman Republic began to **expand** into the lands around it. From 437 to 426 BCE, Rome fought its first major war against a nearby town called Fidenae. Rome then went on to fight and **conquer** a city called Veii in 396 BCE. This city was ruled by a group called the Etruscans.

TAKING OVER ITALY

The city of Rome was established in what is now the country of Italy. The Etruscans and the Greeks already controlled much of Italy by the time the Romans started to expand, so these two **cultures** had a big **influence** on Roman culture.

In 390 BCE, the Romans had to stop expanding their power because they were suddenly attacked by a group called the Gauls. The Gauls agreed to leave after the Romans gave them a lot of gold, but the attack and the payment left Rome weak. It took the Romans 40 years to get their country's strength back.

TAKING ON CARTHAGE

After a series of wars from 340 to 275 BCE, Rome controlled most of Italy and began to look to other parts of the world to conquer. Its first target was Carthage, which was in northern Africa. It was the richest and most powerful city in the **Mediterranean**. The fight between Carthage and Rome lasted 23 years. This was the first war in a set of three, called the Punic Wars. They lasted from 264 to 146 BCE.

A FIERCE ENEMY

For many years, the leader of the Carthaginian army was a man named Hannibal. He is most famous for crossing the Alps, a mountain chain that helped protect the Romans. He and his army, which rode horses and elephants, fought their way through Italy for 15 years. However, Hannibal was never able to conquer Rome. A Roman general named Scipio Africanus finally beat Hannibal in 202 BCE, ending the Second Punic War.

By the end of the First Punic War, Carthage was destroyed and Rome had taken control of the Mediterranean. Before the war started, Rome did not have a navy. It built one to take on Carthage and then used it to further expand its power. The First Punic War also gave Rome the training and wealth it needed to conquer other places with strong militaries. If Rome had lost to Carthage, there would never have been a Roman Empire.

This painting shows a Roman navy boat. The Roman navy played a big part in the growth of Rome into an empire.

THE MACEDONIAN WARS

While fighting Carthage, Rome was also fighting in the four Macedonian Wars. In 214 BCE, King Philip V of Macedonia made an **alliance** with Hannibal of Carthage. This caused Rome to declare war on Macedonia. War continued on and off until 148 BCE. In the Second and Third Macedonian Wars, Rome made an alliance with Greece to fight against Macedonia, which was trying to take over Greece. Each time, Greece and Rome won and the Romans returned to their capital city. After the fourth war, however, the Roman soldiers stayed in Macedonia and made it part of Rome.

This map shows Rome when it was at its largest, using Latin labels.

Over the next few hundred years, Rome kept expanding its power. It was at its largest around 117 CE. It stretched from Egypt to what is now Great Britain. In other words, ancient Rome was about as big as the United States! The Romans built more than 50,000 miles (80,470 kilometers) of roads to connect all the parts of the empire and make it easier for people—especially soldiers—to get around. However, since the main way people got around at that time was by walking or riding horses, it could still take a long time to get anywhere. A website called Orbis tells people today how long it would have taken to get around the Roman Empire at different times of the year and using different ways of getting around. For example, for someone who could not afford to take a boat, getting from London to Jerusalem—two modern cities on lands that were once part of the Roman Empire—could take up to 161 days on foot and more than a year by oxcart!

Rome got much of its wealth from conquering new lands and taxing the people who lived in them, so its army was important. These actors are dressed as ancient Roman soldiers.

CHAPTER THREE

YEARS OF WAR

As Rome grew, most of the attention of the government was on the new lands it was conquering instead of the people inside the republic. Conquered areas, such as those in today's Spain and Greece, brought Rome a lot of wealth. However, instead of spreading that wealth around to all citizens, the government and the army kept it for themselves.

At the same time, the government was forcing ordinary citizens to fight in the Roman army. While they were gone, the rich would buy their land. Soldiers would come back to find that they had to serve someone else on a farm they had once owned. All of these things created a huge gap between the rich and the poor. The patricians had more money than they could spend, while the plebeians were barely surviving.

FIGHTING THE GOVERNMENT

While Rome was fighting people in other lands, its own people were also often fighting against it. The plebeians did not like the way they were treated even before the wealth gap got so large. They did not like the laws that said they could not marry patricians or work for any part of the government except the military. From about 494 to 287 BCE, the plebeians fought for and won more rights, often by going on **strike**. This fight was called the Conflict of the Orders.

Enslaved people also fought against the government. Not much is known about them because people generally ignored them. This means they were almost never written about, so historians do not have a lot of records to get information from. What we do know is that slavery in ancient Rome was not based on race. Instead, enslaved people were mostly people who were conquered by the Romans. Experts believe as many as one-fourth of the people living in Roman lands were enslaved. One of the most famous **rebellions** of enslaved Romans happened from 73 to 71 BCE. It was led by a man named Spartacus. The government won, and the people involved were all killed. However, it scared the Romans because it showed them how strong the enslaved people were when they worked together.

LEARNING FROM HISTORY

Rome had a huge wealth gap, and the wealthy were not paying taxes. Many Romans had lost faith in the government. They believed the patricians cared only about themselves and would not make laws to help the common people. Some senators wanted to help the plebeians so they would vote for them, but a group of rival senators blocked any **reforms** that would have helped people. Many experts say these same things are happening in the United States right now.

The ancient Romans depended on enslaved people to do even the most basic things for them. Shown here are enslaved people carrying someone on a type of bed called a litter.

This statue of Julius Caesar stands next to the remains of the Roman Forum today.

THE FIRST TRIUMVIRATE

Julius Caesar was one of the most famous leaders of Rome. He was elected as a consul in 59 BCE. Caesar, Pompey the Great, and Marcus Crassus formed what is known today as the First Triumvirate, which is a group of three powerful ruling people. Consuls served for only one year, but the Roman Republic was so big by this point that people were needed to rule over different parts of it. The Triumvirate got the Senate to give them five-year terms in what are now the countries of France, Syria, and Spain.

Over time, Caesar and Pompey became enemies and ended up fighting each other from 49 to 45 BCE. Caesar won and returned to Rome, where he declared himself the dictator of Rome for life in 44 BCE. In ancient Rome, a dictator was a leader who had much more power than a consul, but their term was only supposed to last for six months. It was a title that was only meant to be used in times of emergency. On March 15, 44 BCE, Caesar was killed by a group of senators who feared he was becoming too powerful. Experts agree that Caesar's death was a big part of the fall of the Roman Republic.

Octavian (*shown here*) was only 17 years old when Julius Caesar's death made him the ruler of Rome.

CHAPTER FOUR
A PEACEFUL EMPIRE

The Roman Republic had been failing for a long time because of the wealth gap, political fights, and civil wars. After Caesar's death, the civil wars continued as different people fought for power. One of these people was Caesar's grandnephew, Octavian. Caesar had made Octavian his heir before he died because he wanted Octavian to rule Rome after his death. However, Octavian had to defend his title from other people who wanted to take over.

THE SECOND TRIUMVIRATE

Octavian's main rival was a man named Marcus Antonius. His name is often written as Marc Antony. In 43 BCE, the two men called a **truce** and agreed to share power with each other and with a man named Lepidus, who had been one of Caesar's generals. This was the Second Triumvirate. They ruled together until 32 BCE, when they started fighting each other. One of the main reasons for this fight was that Marc Antony was put in charge of the part of Rome that included Egypt, and he fell in love with Egypt's ruler, Cleopatra. She wanted to stay in

This drawing shows Marc Antony meeting Cleopatra in ancient Egypt.

power, but after several years, Octavian challenged her. Antony helped her fight back. Octavian won and made himself the emperor of Rome. The Senate still existed, but it no longer had any real power. It gave Octavian the name Augustus Caesar (sometimes written as Caesar Augustus) in 27 BCE.

REPUBLIC OR EMPIRE?

Even though Rome grew to be huge and ended up including a lot of different countries, it was still a republic until 31 BCE because the main political power was in the Senate, which was made up of many different people. An empire is ruled by one person with all the political power. An emperor is different from a king because an empire is generally made up of many different countries, while a kingdom is just one country with the same culture.

THE PAX ROMANA

Octavian's rule began a 200-year-long period that is now called the Pax Romana, or "Roman peace." During the Pax Romana, the empire was at its largest size. Roman language, politics, law, and other parts of its culture spread across the world. There was peace for its growing number of citizens, and more time and money were spent on the arts. The empire kept its people safe, but it let each part of the empire make its own laws as long as they paid taxes to the emperor. Because people had what they needed to live well and were allowed to make rules they were happy with, the civil wars that had been going on for so long during the Roman Republic stopped.

However, one group did not benefit from the Pax Romana: enslaved people. The empire's focus was on keeping stability in the lands it already had. Since Rome was no longer conquering other places, it was also not getting any new enslaved people. To make sure they had people to work for them, the Romans made laws against freeing those who were already enslaved.

TOO BIG TO BE ONE LAND

By 395 CE, the Roman Empire had become too big, so it split into the Western Empire and the Eastern Empire. The Eastern

This map shows the split between the Roman Empire (*green*) and the Byzantine Empire (*pink*).

Empire became known as the Byzantine Empire. It was ruled by an emperor named Constantine, and it lost much of its original Roman culture. For example, the Romans had always had a polytheistic religion, which meant they worshipped many gods. However, Constantine made Christianity, which only had one god, the official religion of the Byzantine Empire.

Rome continued to rule the Western Empire. In 410 CE, Rome was destroyed by a group of **Germanic** people called the Visigoths. They stole Roman goods and forced many Roman citizens to leave. Over time, the Western Empire started to weaken. Other Germanic tribes from the north began to attack and invade, and Roman leaders began to misuse their power. The Western Empire fell to Germanic tribes in 476 CE. The Eastern Empire, though, remained strong until 1453 CE, when it fell to the Ottoman Empire.

HISTORY HAPPENED HERE

THE COLOSSEUM

- The Colosseum is the largest amphitheater, or round theater, in the world.
- The events held here involved men called gladiators fighting each other or animals.
- Tens of thousands of enslaved people built the Colosseum in the city of Rome from 72 to 80 CE.

HADRIAN'S WALL

- The oldest parts of Hadrian's Wall in England were built around 122 CE, while what's now England was part of the Roman Empire.
- The wall marked the northern border of the empire.
- Today, parts of the wall have fallen down. When it was whole, the wall stretched 73 miles (117 km) across present-day England.

THE PANTHEON

- The Pantheon was a temple that was built in the city of Rome to honor all the gods the Romans worshipped.
- It is the ancient Roman building that is in the best shape.
- No one knows the exact age of the Pantheon, but experts believe the original structure was built around 27 BCE.

EVENTS DURING ANCIENT ROME

753 BCE Rome is created by Romulus, a mythical king.

509 BCE Rome becomes a republic.

494 BCE The plebeians start fighting for their rights in the Conflict of the Orders.

CA. 450 BCE The written set of laws called the Twelve Tables is created.

437 BCE The Romans start expanding into surrounding Italy.

264–146 BCE Rome fights the Punic Wars.

73–71 BCE Spartacus leads a rebellion of enslaved people.

59 BCE Julius Caesar is elected consul.

45–44 BCE Julius Caesar defeats Pompey and declares himself dictator for life.

44 BCE Julius Caesar is killed by Roman senators.

43 BCE The Second Triumvirate is formed.

31 BCE Octavian (later called Augustus Caesar) becomes emperor. The Roman Empire replaces the Roman Republic.

27 BCE The Pax Romana, a period of peace and growth in Rome, begins and lasts for about 200 years.

395 CE The Roman Empire splits into the Western Empire and the Eastern, or Byzantine, Empire.

476 CE The Western Empire falls after attacks by Germanic tribes.

GLOSSARY

alliance: People, groups, or countries working together for a specific purpose.

archaeologist: Someone who studies the tools and other objects left behind by ancient people.

conquer: To take by force.

culture: The beliefs and ways of life of a group of people.

expand: To make larger.

Germanic: A term used by ancient Romans for peoples living in northern central Europe.

influence: To have an effect on.

Mediterranean: A sea between Europe and Africa as well as the area surrounding this sea.

rebellion: An open fight against authority.

reform: An improvement made by removing faults or problems.

strike: To stop work in order to force an authority to meet demands.

truce: An agreement to stop fighting.

FIND OUT MORE

BOOKS

Bell, Samantha. *Ancient Rome*. Lake Elmo, MN: Focus Readers, 2020.

Loh-Hagan, Virginia. *Ancient Rome*. Ann Arbor, MI: 45th Parallel Press, 2021.

Nicholson, Sue. *Ancient Rome*. New York, NY: DK Publishing, 2020.

WEBSITES

DK Find Out!: Ancient Rome
www.dkfindout.com/us/history/ancient-rome
This interactive website offers information about Roman buildings, people, towns, and more.

Ducksters: Ancient Rome for Kids
www.ducksters.com/history/ancient_rome.php
This website contains articles covering many topics about ancient Rome, including its religion, important people, and culture.

The School Run: Roman Life and Culture
www.theschoolrun.com/homework-help/roman-life-and-culture
This website gives information and fun facts about ancient Rome.

Publisher's note to educators and parents: Our editors have carefully reviewed these websites to ensure that they are suitable for students. Many websites change frequently, however, and we cannot guarantee that a site's future contents will continue to meet our high standards of quality and educational value. Be advised that students should be closely supervised whenever they access the internet.

INDEX